THE BUG HANDBOOK

KELLY GAUTHIER

APPLESAUCE · PRESS

KENNEBUNKPORT, MAINE

13-Digit ISBN: 978-1604338027
10-Digit ISBN: 1604338024

This book may be ordered by mail from the publisher. Please include $5.99 for postage and handling.
Please support your local bookseller first!

Books published by Cider Mill Press Book Publishers are available at special discounts for bulk purchases in the United States by corporations, institutions, and other organizations. For more information, please contact the publisher.

Applesauce Press is an imprint of
Cider Mill Press Book Publishers
"Where good books are ready for press"
PO Box 454
12 Spring Street
Kennebunkport, Maine 04046

Visit us online!
www.cidermillpress.com

Cover and interior design by Annalisa Sheldahl
Typography: Destroy, Gipsiero, PMN Caecilia, Block Berthold

Image Credits: All artwork by Julius Csotonyi. All vectors used under official license by Shutterstock.com.

Printed in China

1 2 3 4 5 6 7 8 9 0
First Edition

CONTENTS

WHAT ARE BUGS?

In this book, we define a "bug" as a type of animal with a hard outer body (exoskeleton), a segmented body and legs, and no backbone (invertebrate). Some scientists argue that only certain types of insects are "true bugs," but we're going to use that term in a general sense and look at a group of animals called "arthropods."

The number of body and leg segments varies from bug to bug. Spiders have two body sections and eight legs. Insects have three body sections and six legs. Some bugs have many body sections and many legs. The number of sections and legs determines a bug's species and class.

Some bugs, including bees and wasps, can fly, while others—including centipedes and caterpillars—move around by crawling.

A type of jumping spider, the peacock spider has a unique dance where it wiggles its third pair of legs to get attention.

HOW MANY BUGS ARE THERE IN THE WORLD?

Entomology is the scientific study of bugs. Entomologists have identified hundreds of thousands of different species, and they believe there may be millions more to discover.

Scientists estimate that there are about 10 quintillion (that's 10 followed by 18 zeros!) individual bugs living in the world. Compare that to the 7 billion (7 followed by 9 zeros) people on the planet, and it's pretty clear that there are a lot more bugs than humans!

A bulldog ant (right) battles a wasp. Because both can sting, this fight may seem evenly matched, but the bulldog ant's strong pincers give it an advantage.

HOW LONG DO BUGS LIVE?

During its life, a bug goes through as many as four developmental stages and generally begins life as an egg. Most bugs have a lifespan of less than a year because they survive as adults for only one season. Some bugs, however, can live for many years!

A bug's protective hard outer body (exoskeleton) helps it survive. Some bugs use wings to fly away from predators, while others choose a hard-to-reach habitat that keeps them safe. Bugs can also use their stingers to keep predators away.

THREE-STAGE LIFE CYCLE

Spiders, grasshoppers, and some insects begin life as an egg, hatch into a young form called a "nymph," and grow into adults. Nymphs and adults look alike, so it can be hard to tell them apart!

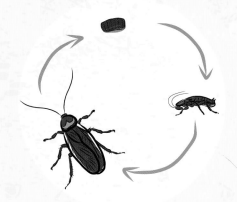

FOUR-STAGE LIFE CYCLE

The lives of beetles, butterflies, and many other winged bugs have four stages, including a full metamorphosis. They begin as an egg, hatch into larva, and then move into the pupa stage, where they get covered in a protective skin that allows them to develop. Some of these skins are thin and allow the pupa to move around, but others are thick like the cocoon of a moth. After the pupa stage, the bug grows wings and finishes its metamorphosis into an adult.

13

HOW SMALL ARE BUGS?

Bugs come in all shapes and sizes. Some are so small the human eye can barely see them, such as the fairyfly wasp, which measures a mere ⅕ millimeter. And there are bugs, such as giant centipedes, that can be as long as 30 centimeters. That's an entire foot.

The average body can be anywhere from 5 to 6 millimeters (¼ inch) to 5 to 6 centimeters (2 inches). Bugs with long legs or wings are much larger if you measure their legspan or wingspan as well as their body.

Compare the size of an ant, which can grow up to 25 millimeters (1 inch) in some species, to the size of a tarantula, which can have a legspan of up to 28 centimeters (11 inches). Bug sizes can vary a lot!

In comparison to humans, bugs are tiny. Take that same tarantula and put it next to us, a 175-centimeter (5 foot, 9 inch) human. The tarantula may be large for a bug, but its whole body is only ¹⁄₁₆ the size of ours.

5 FEET, 9 INCHES

11 INCHES

1 INCH

WHERE DO BUGS LIVE?

he short answer—everywhere! Bugs are found on every continent on the planet, and some bugs are even found in water.

Most bugs are ground or tree dwellers, and will live in gardens or forests their entire lives. Gardeners and farmers in particular will notice lots of bugs on flowers, fruits, and vegetables, since many bugs use these for food. Plenty of bugs are burrowers and live in holes under the ground. Ants, for example, live protected under the surface and enter their homes through anthills.

Some bugs can swim and lay their eggs in water. There are even certain types of bugs, such as sea spiders, that spend most of their lives in the water.

Although bugs survive longest in warmer weather, there are species that live in the Arctic and Antarctic. They're usually only active in the summer months, just like countless other bugs in milder climates.

Of course, some bugs make their way into homes, especially when the weather gets colder. Some species, termites for example, can damage homes. But others, such as ladybugs and spiders, simply come to visit. They're annoying guests, but they won't do much harm.

The pycnogonid, commonly known as sea spider, can't spin a web but it can live up to 52 feet under the sea!

WHAT DO BUGS EAT?

Common garden bugs are typically plant eaters (herbivores), feeding on leaves, grass, seeds, nectar, and sap. Bugs that can chew, such as beetles and grasshoppers, eat solid foods like leaves, grass, and even wood. Bugs with a long, tongue-like tube for a mouth, such as butterflies and bees, usually suck up nectar or sap from flowers.

Not all bugs are herbivores. Lots of bugs eat other bugs. The dragonfly, praying mantis, and spider are all predators that eat other insects, and there are also species that have been known to eat larger prey such as small frogs, fish, lizards, or even birds.

Ticks and mosquitoes, along with some other bugs, are known as "parasites" because they feed on blood as their main food source.

A tiger beetle catches and
eats a small bee.

WHICH BUGS ARE ENDANGERED?

In 2016, the International Union for Conservation of Nature (IUCN) listed about 250 species of insects and spiders as "critically endangered." The IUCN also listed more than 500 species as "endangered" and more than 650 species as "vulnerable." Bugs, like all other animals, rely on their habitats to help them survive. If their home is threatened or their food source is taken away, they struggle.

In the United States, the U.S. Fish & Wildlife Service is responsible for declaring a species "endangered," which allows that species to be legally protected. In early 2017, the bumble bee made headlines when a particular species, the rusty patched bumble bee, was declared endangered due to a large decline in population caused by lost habitat, disease, and pesticides.

The Gooty Sapphire Tarantula is listed as "critically endangered" by the IUCN.

WHAT BUGS ARE DANGEROUS?

While lots of bugs are perfectly harmless, some will try to protect themselves if they feel threatened.

STINGING BUGS

Some bugs have stingers that allow them to quickly sting and release a small amount of venom that causes pain or burning. Common stinging bugs are bees, wasps, and hornets. Some ants, such as fire ants, also have stingers. Some caterpillars, such as the flannel moth and saddleback caterpillars, sting through hairs that look similar to fur but are actually quill-like spines.

WHEN IS A STING DANGEROUS?

Because bugs are so small, most stings are not dangerous unless there is a swarm of the bugs, such as a hornet's nest, or if the person stung has an allergic reaction to the venom. Some ants are able to sting multiple times, which can also be dangerous.

BITING BUGS

Lots of bugs will bite when threatened or searching for food. Their bites can often leave a raised or red bump. Mosquitos, ticks, lice, bed bugs, and fleas are all common parasites that feed on blood, and their bites can be very itchy. Some species of spiders, flies, and ants—such as carpenter ants—can bite, as can chiggers, centipedes, and water bugs. Unlike a painful sting, you may not even feel a bug bite.

WHEN IS A BITE DANGEROUS?

As with stings, bug bites can be dangerous if you are allergic. Most bug bites from parasites are itchy and annoying, but not necessarily dangerous. Some spiders, such as black widows and brown recluse spiders, have strong venom that can be harmful if left untreated. Parasites are a problem because they can carry diseases, so the bite may go away, but other symptoms could appear later.

WHY DO SOME BUGS MIGRATE?

Since bugs struggle in the cold, they will often move as a group to warmer areas when the seasons change. Many dragonfly, beetle, butterfly, and moth species migrate. Because bugs have such short lifespans, a migration might take place over a few generations. An adult bug may travel to lay its eggs while the new generation makes the return trip, stopping to lay the eggs that will become the next generation of migrating adults.

For example, monarch butterflies are well known for their migration across North America. The monarchs may take as many as 4 or 5 generations to complete a full migration cycle from Canada to Mexico and back to Canada.

Male orchid bees smell particularly good. They are very attracted to the scent of orchids and will gather the oils from the flower so that they smell just as wonderful!

WHAT ARE SOME COMMON TYPES OF BUGS?

Because there are so many species of bugs in the world, it's impossible to cover them all. What you see in your backyard will vary based on where you live, but here are a few common types to look for.

ANTS

Ants live in colonies made up of different classes, including worker ants, soldiers, and a queen. Some ants are winged. Some bite or sting to keep away predators. While they may be small, ants can carry anywhere from 10 to 50 times their own weight.

BEES

Bees are pollinators that help flowers and crops grow. They're found on every continent except Antarctica, where it's too cold for them to survive. Some of the most common types are honey bees and bumblebees, both recognizable by their yellow and black fur.

26

BEETLES

When beetles want to fly, their distinctive hard outer shells (elytra) lift so that their wings can move. Some beetles, such as the rhinoceros beetle, have horns and can defend themselves. Other beetles, like stink bugs, will let off a terrible smell when disturbed.

BUTTERFLIES

Like bees, butterflies are pollinators that help plants and flowers grow, but these beautiful bugs are best known for their wings, which come in a variety of shapes, sizes, and patterns.

CATERPILLARS

Caterpillars are the larval stage of butterflies and moths. As these long-bodied, many-legged bugs develop, they undergo a metamorphosis, grow wings, and become adults. While in the caterpillar stage, these bugs come in different colors and patterns—some caterpillars even have furry bodies!

CENTIPEDES

Centipedes have long bodies with one pair of legs per segment, and they always have an odd number of leg pairs. Despite their name, centipedes don't always have 100 pairs of legs. A close cousin is the millipede, which has two pairs of legs per body segment.

COCKROACHES

Not only do these common bugs have very tough bodies, which allowed them to survive from ancient times to the present, but they also tend to travel in groups.

DRAGONFLIES

Dragonflies' long, stick-like bodies and two pairs of wings make them very fast fliers. Their usual habitat is near water. Nymphs often live in the water for months or even years. Dragonflies are typically carnivores.

FLIES

Flies are unique among flying bugs because they have only one pair of wings, instead of the usual two. Flies can be helpful pollinators, but some types, such as mosquitos, are biting nuisances that may spread disease.

GRASSHOPPERS

If you've ever tried to catch a grasshopper, you'll know that their name comes from their ability to leap long distances. Not just for jumping, those powerful legs allow grasshoppers to produce their distinctive chirping noise.

MANTIS

The mantis is known for its long front legs, which are very useful for catching prey. They have lengthy necks and bodies, and some species have wings. One of the most common types is the praying mantis.

MOTHS

Similar to butterflies, moths are winged, flying bugs. But, most moth species are nocturnal, meaning you'll only see them at night. Scientists don't know exactly why, but moths are very attracted to artificial lights.

SPIDERS

Spider bodies have two segments and eight legs. The come in all different shapes and sizes, from the tiniest of garden spiders to the tarantulas of the jungle. Spiders are known for making thin, silky webs to catch their prey. Special glands at the tip of their abdomen produce this silky thread.

WASPS

Wasps are flying insects similar to bees and ants. While some wasps, like yellow jackets and hornets, live in colonies, other species live alone. Wasps date back to the prehistoric period.

The ruby-tailed wasp is capable of curli
up in a ball to protect itself from sting
from other types of wasps and bees.

SPECIES TO SEARCH FOR

Everyone can be a bug hunter! Get out your magnifying glass and camera and see how many of these common critters you can spot. These species are common to large regions of the world, so if you can't find them in your own yard you might be able to spot them one day while you're traveling. You'll be able to see some of the larger ones with your own eyes, such as moths or butterflies, but you may have to search around the ground or trees for the smaller species. Always be careful when you're out in nature, because not all plants are safe to touch. Try keeping a log of the different species you see and the locations you find them in. You might find that some of bugs are frequent visitors to your favorite places!

This bug is classified as "invasive"
in North America and Australia.

32

COMMON EUROPEAN EARWIG
(*FORFICULA AURICULARIA*)

WHERE: North America, Europe, and western Asia

SIZE: 12–20 millimeters (about ½ inch)

LOOK FOR: Reddish-brown color, flat body, and pincers on the end of the body

BUG BITE: Despite the name, earwigs don't live in ears. In fact, they can live in a wide variety of environments and are found in many different parts of the world. These distinctive little insects have pincers at the end of their bodies, and the males generally have larger and more curved pincers than the females. Although they can fly, common earwigs rarely do.

These bugs can be a real pest. They mostly come out at night and take shelter in dark, damp places. They can be very invasive if they take up residence in a house and will get into everything including floorboards, household plants, pantries, and even furniture and clothing.

RAINBOW DUNG BEETLE
(*PHANAEUS VINDEX*)

WHERE: North America

SIZE: 1–2 centimeters

LOOK FOR: Metallic green, yellow, and red body

BUG BITE: The rainbow dung beetle is named for the rainbow of colors covering its body. It is part of a family of bugs called "scarab beetles," which used to be worshiped in ancient Egypt. The males have a large horn on the front of their head. The "dung" part of the beetle's name comes from where it is born. This beetle will tunnel under a pile of dung to lay their eggs.

ANTLION
(EUROLEON NOSTRAS)

WHERE: All over the world, but prefer warmer climates

SIZE: 12–15 centimeter (4½–6 inch) wingspan

LOOK FOR: Two pairs of narrow wings (similar to a dragonfly) in adults; small body with three pairs of legs and pincers at the head in larvae

BUG BITE: These bugs have a four-stage life cycle from egg to larva (young) to cocoon to adult. While the adult antlion is nocturnal and very similar to a dragonfly, the larva antlion is a ferocious bug. The young antlions are ambush predators and will conceal themselves in a funnel-like pit and wait for prey, particularly ants, to fall in.

The antlion larva is also sometimes called the "doodlebug" because the way it travels leaves a winding trail.

An ant (left) falls into the pit of the antlion larva (right).

MONARCH BUTTERFLY
(*DANAUS PLEXIPPUS*)

WHERE: North America and northern South America

SIZE: 8–12 centimeter (3–4 inches) wingspan

LOOK FOR: Orange wings with black lines and white spots

BUG BITE: The monarch butterfly is one of the most recognizable types of butterflies. It has a life cycle with four stages in it. The first stage of their life is the egg, which is laid on a milkweed plant. The eggs hatch into caterpillars just about four days after they are laid, and the caterpillars spend two weeks growing. Then, the caterpillar will use silk to create a chrysalis, or cocoon, where it changes into a butterfly. After about 10 days in the cocoon, the fully grown monarch butterfly emerges.

Monarch butterflies are most well-known for their migration. Every fall, the monarch butterflies migrate from their home in North America to South America to live out the winter months. Fascinatingly, the butterflies only live long enough to make the journey once in their lives, so it is unclear how the new butterflies know where to go each year.

RED-AND-BLACK STRIPED STINK BUG
(GRAPHOSOMA LINEATUM)

WHERE: Parts of Europe, western Asia, and North Africa

SIZE: 8–12 millimeters

LOOK FOR: Red and black stripes on the body

BUG BITE: This bug is also known as a type of "shield bug," because the striped section of their body acts as a shield to protect them from predators. Their colors act as a warning to oncoming predators as well, because these bugs do not taste good. That's why they are called "stink bugs." The striped stink bug prefers dry climates and will hide in trees when the weather is bad.

38

SPILOMYIA FLY
(*SPILOMYIA LONGICORNIS*)

WHERE: North America

SIZE: 10–15 millimeters (about ½ inch)

LOOK FOR: Black and yellow striped body, two wings

BUG BITE: This fly is great at pretending to be a bee. It will hover in the air or over flowers and make buzzing noises, and its yellow and black body looks like a wasp or yellow jacket. These flies eat mostly pollen and nectar. Although their bee imitation might fool predators into staying away, they cannot sting like bees can.

One way to distinguish these flies from bees is to look at their wings. Flies only have two wings, while bees have four.

YUCCA MOTH
(*TEGETICULA YUCCASELLA*)

WHERE: Southwestern United States and Mexico

SIZE: 2–3 centimeter (1 inch) wingspan

LOOK FOR: White or silvery wings

BUG BITE: The yucca moth lives in harmony with the yucca plant, and they could not exist without each other. The female moth's main job is to pollinate the yucca flower, and she will always lay eggs within the yucca flower. In return, the yucca flower is the only source of food for yucca moth larvae.

The yucca moth has a specially developed mouth that looks like tentacles, which helps it collect and transport the yucca flower's pollen from plant to plant. This process only happens at night.

*A female yucca moth pollinates
a yucca flower in the moonlight.*

GIANT PILL MILLIPEDE

(SPHAEROTHERIUM GIGANTEUM)

WHERE: Southern and southeast Asia, southern Africa, Australia

SIZE: 1–3 centimeters (1–3 inches)

LOOK FOR: Black body with red plates

BUG BITE: This bug has a great defense. The outer part of the giant pill millipede's body is hard for protection. When they feel threatened, these bugs roll up into a ball. The tail of the pill millipede wraps all the way around and covers its head, making a perfectly round armor. When rolled up, these giant bugs are typically about the same size as a golf ball, although some have been known to be as big as a baseball.

LEICHHARDT'S GRASSHOPPER
(PETASIDA EPHIPPIGERA)

WHERE: Australia

SIZE: 5–7 centimeters (2–2½ inches)

LOOK FOR: Orange body with blue and black spots

BUG BITE: These grasshoppers prefer to eat a minty-smelling, but bitter-tasting, plant called "pityrodia," and will often live on just one bush for their entire lives. Thanks to the bitter taste of the pityrodia bush, these grasshoppers taste terrible, so they are less likely to become prey!

43

BROAD-WINGED KATYDID
(MICROCENTRUM RHOMBIFOLIUM)

WHERE: Southwestern and eastern United States (excluding New England)

SIZE: 5–6 centimeters (about 2 inches)

LOOK FOR: Wide, green wings

BUG BITE: The katydid likes shady areas and is often found in forests or areas with lots of leaves and shrubs. As a disguise, the katydid's green wings are angled and covered in veins, which makes them look like a small leaf. You might hear this bug before you see it. The katydid has a very recognizable call that sounds like a repeated ticking noise and lasts for a few seconds at a time.

HARLEQUIN LADYBEETLE
(HARMONIA AXYRIDIS)

WHERE: Asia, North America, South America, Europe, South Africa

SIZE: 5½–8½ millimeters

LOOK FOR: Red body with black spots

BUG BITE: The harlequin ladybeetle is more commonly known as a "ladybug." The markings on the ladybeetle can vary. Ladybeetles can be very helpful in the wild because they feed on bugs known as "plant lice," which can be harmful to plants and crops. But, these beetles can also become a problem for houses. Because they don't like the cold months, ladybeetles often invade homes in the winter. Like other beetles, they will release a smell and fluid when frightened or threatened to scare off predators. Ladybeetles are said to be good luck.

EMPEROR SCORPION
(PANDINUS IMPERATOR)

WHERE: Western Africa

SIZE: 20 centimeters (8 inches)

LOOK FOR: Dark body, two front pincers, and a long, curved tail

BUG BITE: The emperor scorpion lives in both rainforests and savannas, where it burrows into the soil beneath rocks and leaves. The body of a scorpion is hard for protection and has a metallic shine. In fact, emperor scorpions will glow under ultraviolet light.

Their curved tail has a special stinger filled with venom that helps the scorpion paralyze its prey. Although they may look intimidating, these scorpions are fairly harmless to humans. A scorpion sting is similar to a bee sting. It may hurt, but it usually won't cause much of a reaction unless the victim is allergic to the venom.

*Their front pincers aren't just for show;
they help this scorpion catch and hold
onto insects, mice, and lizards.*

LIGHTNING BUG

(PHOTINUS PYRALIS)

WHERE: North America

SIZE: 10–15 millimeters

LOOK FOR: Red head, black body, and yellow or "lit" tail area

BUG BITE: Another common name for this bug is the "firefly," and if you've ever seen it at night you know why. Though it can be known as a fly, this bug is actually a type of beetle. They are most easily spotted as the sun is going down, when they use a special organ on the lower part of their body to flash light patterns. These patterns of light help the lightning bugs to find one another at night. However, their lights can also attract predators, so lightning bugs need to have a great defense. To protect themselves, lightning bugs will release a bad smell or a sticky substance when a predator attacks.

GOLIATH BEETLE
(GOLIATHUS GOLIATUS)

WHERE: Africa

SIZE: 5–10 centimeters (2–4 inches)

LOOK FOR: Dark brown body, black head with white stripes

BUG BITE: This large beetle is named after the biblical Goliath for its size. The Goliath beetle is one of the largest types of beetles and can sometimes grow to be as large as a small bird. These beetles have a pair of wings that stay tucked underneath their body until they need to travel. Male Goliath beetles have a Y-shaped horn at the end of their heads. Most often, they use this horn to fight with other Goliath beetles over food or mates.

   The Goliath beetle typically lives in forest or savanna areas, so its main food is tree sap and fruit common to its habitat.

NORTHERN MOLE CRICKET
(*NEOCURTILLA HEXADACTYLA*)

WHERE: Eastern North America

SIZE: 2–3 centimeters (about 1 inch)

LOOK FOR: Brown, hard body

BUG BITE: The front legs of the mole cricket are flattened and adapted for burrowing. Much like the mole it is named for, the mole cricket will burrow deep into muddy ground near lakes and streams. These crickets have a low-pitched chirp and will call from their burrows.

    As protection, the mole cricket is able to release a slimy substance to fight off predators.

WASP MANTIDFLY
(*CLIMACIELLA BRUNNEA*)

WHERE: North America

SIZE: 2–3 centimeters (about 1 inch)

LOOK FOR: Black body with yellow stripes

BUG BITE: This bug may look like a wasp with its black and yellow body, but this appearance is a disguise. This bug is a predator and uses the fact that it looks like a wasp to its advantage. The wasp mantidfly hovers around flowers to set its trap. When another bug mistakes it for a wasp and gets too close, the mantidfly uses its front two legs to snatch its prey out of the air.

HERCULES BEETLE
(DYNASTES HERCULES)

WHERE: Central and South America

SIZE: Males up to 18 centimeters, females up to 7 centimeters

LOOK FOR: Yellow body, large black horn in males

BUG BITE: The Hercules beetle is named after the ancient Greek figure for its impressive size and strength. In fact, it is the third largest beetle known. This beetle is characterized as a rhinocerous beetle beause of the large black horn on the males. These horns allow them to carry food and objects that are 80 times heavier than the beetle itself.

This beetle only lives as an adult for a few months, but it will remain in its larval stage for up to two years, surviving mainly on rotting wood. It is capable of flying but is more likely to be found on the mossy ground of the forest, hunting for fallen fruit or leaves to eat.

A Hercules beetle rests on the moss next to a poison dart frog.

TRUE OR FALSE

1. A bug's hard outer body is called an "exoskeleton." **T/F**

2. There are not very many bugs in the world. **T/F**

3. Bugs do not lay eggs. **T/F**

4. All bugs have a four-stage life cycle. **T/F**

5. A fairyfly wasp is a very small type of bug. **T/F**

6. Bugs cannot survive in the water.　　　T/F

7. All bugs are herbivores.　　　T/F

8. The rusty patched bumble bee is endangered.　　　T/F

9. Caterpillars can sting.　　　T/F

10. Bugs migrate in groups.　　　T/F

About the Author

Kelly Gauthier is a writer, researcher, editor, and enthusiast of animals big and small. Her love of bugs started at a young age with a bug-collecting kit, which sent her to the backyard to collect caterpillars, worms, and "roly-poly" bugs, and she is incredibly grateful to her parents for always indulging her butterfly obsession. When she doesn't have her nose buried in a book, she is most likely to be found talking about bugs with the talented team at Cider Mill Press. She is based in Boston.

She is also the author of *Discovering Bugs*.

About the Illustrator

Julius Csotonyi is one of the world's most high-profile and talented contemporary scientific illustrators. His considerable academic expertise informs his stunning, dynamic art. He has created life-sized dinosaur murals for the Royal Ontario Museum and for the Dinosaur Hall at the Natural History Museum of Los Angeles County as well as most of the artwork for the new Hall of Paleontology at the Houston Museum of Natural Science. He lives in Canada.

His books include *Discovering Sharks*, *The T. Rex Handbook*, *The Paleoart of Julius Csotonyi*, and *Prehistoric Predators*.

About Applesauce Press

Good ideas ripen with time. From seed to harvest, Applesauce Press crafts books with beautiful designs, creative formats, and kid-friendly information on a variety of fascinating topics. Like our parent company, Cider Mill Press Book Publishers, our press bears fruit twice a year, publishing a new crop of titles each spring and fall.

KENNEBUNKPORT, MAINE

Write to us at:
PO Box 454
Kennebunkport, ME 04046

Or visit us online at:
cidermillpress.com